Disney PRINCESS

Princess

Annual 2013

This Disney Princess Annual belongs to

REBECCA

....

Write your name here

Disney Princess

Meet the Princesses   8

Cinderella

Celebrate with Cinderella   10

Story: Forgotten Friends   12

Princess Present   16

Helpful Friends   17

Royal Celebration   18

Rapunzel

Celebrate with Rapunzel   20

Story: The Party Picture   22

Magical Message   24

Pretty Rapunzel   25

Princess Gift Bag   26

Lovely Lights   27

Belle

Celebrate with Belle   28

Story: The Secret Garden   30

Magical Match   32

Belle's Ball Gown   33

Enchanted Ballroom   34

Tiana and Jasmine

Celebrate with Tiana and Jasmine   36
Enchanting Puzzles   38

Ariel

Celebrate with Ariel   40
Story: The Lost Voices   42
Ocean Gifts   44
Underwater Fun   45
Royal Concert   46

Aurora

Celebrate with Aurora   48
Story: A Starry Night   50
Love Song   52
Party Hat   53
Princess Puzzles   54

Snow White

Celebrate with Snow White   56
Story: The Forest Princess   58
Princess Teasers   60
Tea Party Puzzle   62
Royal Dance   63

Party Time   64
Princess Poster   66
Answers   67

Meet the Princesses

Rapunzel

Rapunzel is full of energy and loves exploring the world outside her tower.

Snow White

Snow White looks after the seven dwarfs. She is kind, caring and gentle.

Ariel

Ariel is kind-hearted and curious. She collects objects that she finds under the sea.

Cinderella

Cinderella is kind and caring. Her fairy godmother grants her magical wishes.

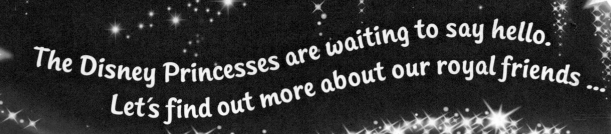

The Disney Princesses are waiting to say hello.
Let's find out more about our royal friends ...

★ Jasmine

Jasmine is brave and adventurous. She loves flying to faraway places.

★ Belle

Gentle Belle is a thoughtful princess. She lives in a castle with the Beast.

★ Aurora

Aurora is loving and caring. Her best friends are the forest animals.

★ Tiana

Tiana is kind and thoughtful. She works hard to make her dreams come true.

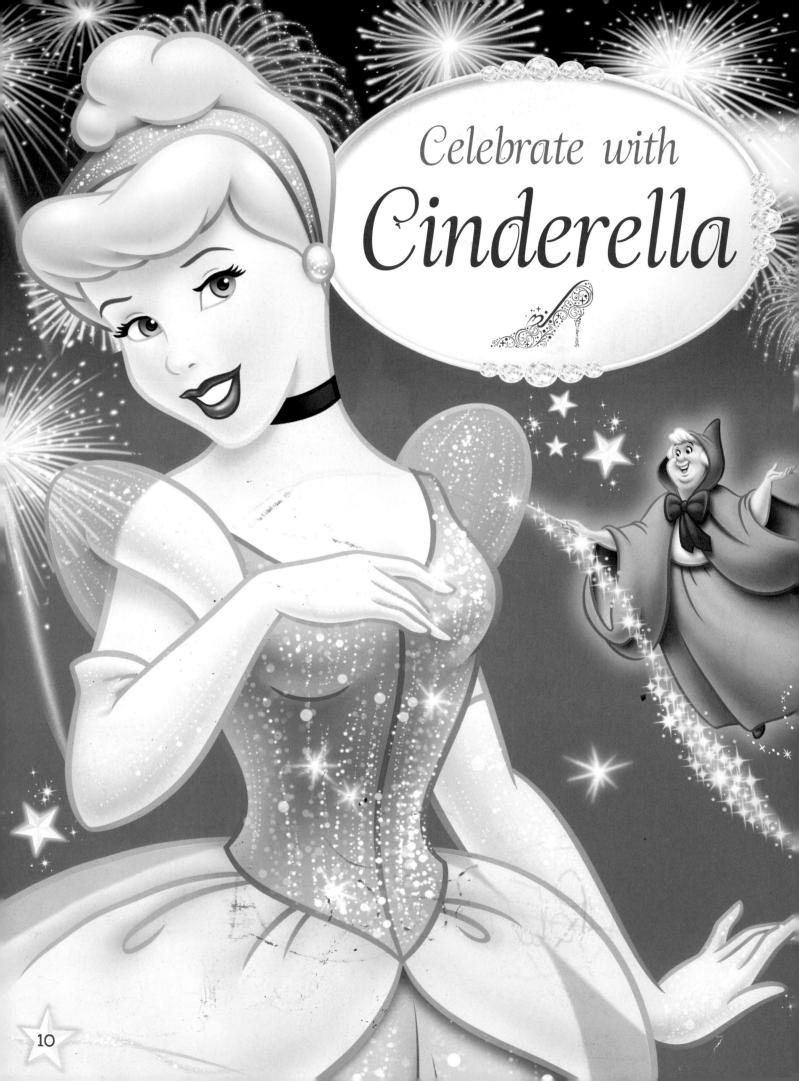

Celebrate with
Cinderella

Cinderella loves all kinds of royal celebrations.
Read on to discover more ...

Magical Dress

When Cinderella went to her first ball, her fairy godmother used magic to create a beautiful ball gown.

Colour Cinderella and her prince.

Special Friends

Cinderella loves planning parties for her mice friends. She even makes tiny outfits for them to wear!

Birthday Surprise

When it's Prince Charming's birthday, Cinderella always thinks up a special surprise for him.

Forgotten Friends

1 Cinderella was planning a grand ball at the palace, with a spectacular fireworks display. Gus and Jaq wanted to help their friend, so they decided to make her a surprise ball gown.

2 Prince Charming had a surprise of his own, too! He gave Cinderella a gift. "I wonder what's inside?".. thought Gus, as he watched from behind a curtain.

3 The gift was a ball gown that once belonged to the Prince's mother. "It's to wear tonight," the Prince told Cinderella. "I would be delighted to!" Cinderella replied.

4 Well, even a mouse knows that a princess cannot wear two ball gowns to a ball! So Gus told the other mice what he had seen.

5 "Now that Cinderella's a princess, I don't think she needs our help anymore," Gus cried. All the mice agreed that it was time to leave the palace and find a new home.

6 While no-one was looking, the mice left the palace. "We're just Cinderella's forgotten friends." said Gus, sadly.

13

7 Later, Cinderella found the ball gown that the mice had been making for her. "My friends must have been upset when they heard I would wear the Queen's dress to the ball," she said.

8 Cinderella searched the whole palace for her mouse friends. She eventually found them out in the muddy gardens. "Please don't go," Cinderella called to them.

9 "You don't need our help anymore," Gus said. "You don't have friends just because you need their help," Cinderella replied. "You treasure them because you adore them."

10 Cinderella insisted that the mice stay at the palace and she invited them to the ball. She even made new clothes for them to wear.

11 The ball began with a bang as fireworks lit up the sky. The guests gasped as they watched the spectacular display.

12 The mice could hardly believe their eyes when the fireworks exploded into giant mouse shapes! "Cinderella planned the fireworks right from the start," Gus giggled. "She never forgot her friends!"

The End

Princess Present

Which gift will Cinderella give to her friend?
Follow the ribbons to find out.

a

b

c

Start

Answer on page 67.

Helpful Friends

Cinderella's friends are adding the finishing touches to her dress. Can you add some colour?

Can you count five mice? Colour the glass slipper once you've found them all.

Royal Celebration

Cinderella is planning a celebration at the palace. Can you help her by completing these party puzzles?

Colourful Gown

Cross out the letters that appear twice, to reveal what colour dress Cinderella will wear to the party.

Write the colour of Cinderella's dress below.

f p d e
e f i
n k d

K _ _ _ _ (Kind)

Pretty Rapunzel

Use the small picture to help you colour this pretty image of Rapunzel.

Which two flowers are exactly the same?

a

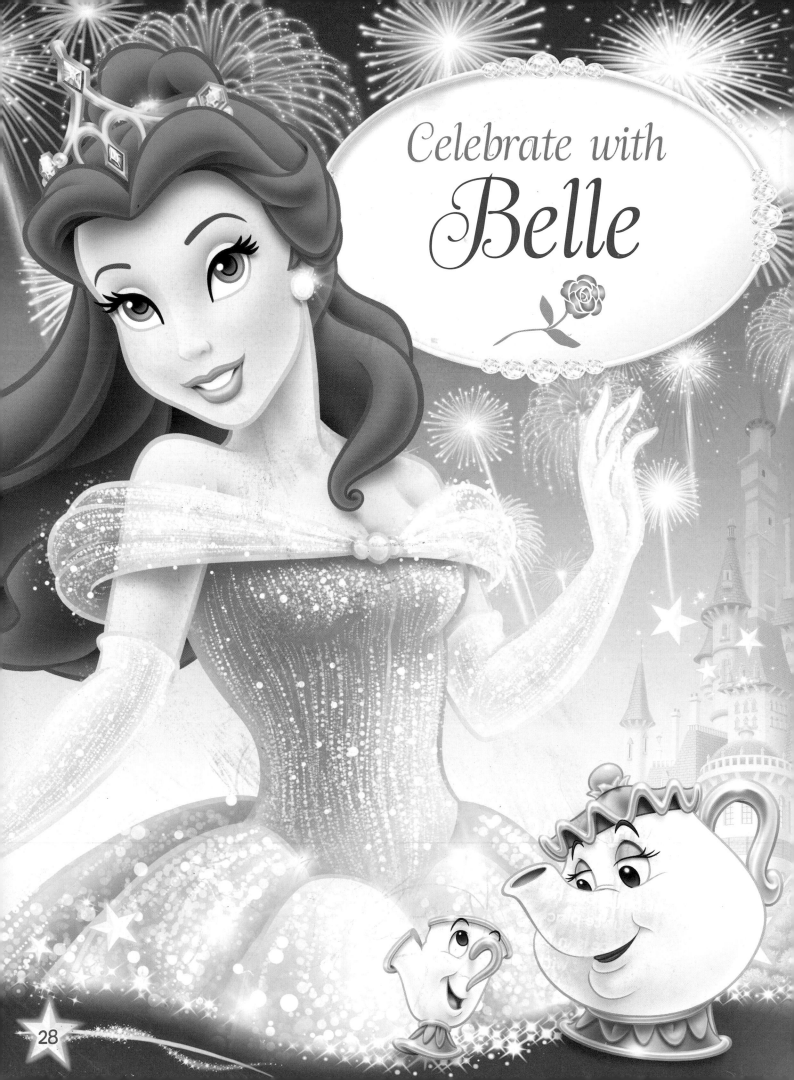

Celebrate with *Belle*

Belle loves preparing for celebrations and surprises. Let's find out more ...

Magical Dress

Belle enjoys baking. She likes to make yummy cakes and biscuits for princess tea parties.

Colour Belle and the Beast.

Perfect Dress

The Wardrobe always makes sure Belle has something special to wear for every royal occasion.

Moonlit Dance

Belle loves dancing at balls, but her favourite place to dance is in the moonlight with the Beast.

The Secret Garden

1 It was Belle's birthday and the Beast could hardly wait to give Belle his present – it was a special key!

t colour is apunzel's dress?

e

2 The Beast led Belle into the castle garden. "I wonder what this key is for?" she asked, excitedly.

3 The Beast took Belle to a gate hidden at the side of the castle. Belle had never noticed it before.

4 The gate opened to reveal a secret garden! As the Beast handed Belle a rose, something magical happened ...

5 The garden transformed into a wonderful party. Belle was wearing a beautiful gown and all of her friends were there. "Thank you, Beast," Belle said. "This is the best birthday present ever."

The End

Magical Match

Belle looks beautiful. Can you match the close-ups in the hearts to the big picture?

a

b

c

d

e

Which close-up doesn't appear in the picture?

Answer on page 67.

Belle's Ball Gown

The Wardrobe has created a beautiful dress for Belle.
Can you finish it by adding a pretty pattern?

See if you can spot
Mrs Potts and Chip!

yes

Answer on page 67.

Enchanted Ballroom

Belle and the Beast are having a party with their enchanted friends.

1

How many friends are at the party in total? Trace over the correct number.

or

2 Unscramble the letters below to reveal what Belle and the Beast are doing?

d a n i n c g

Write your answer below. The first letter is written for you.

d a n c i n g

3 Which two friends are also dancing at the party? *a* and *b*

a

b

c

4 Can you spot Belle's book in the room? *Yes*

5 I can count 5 red petals.

Answers on page 67.

36

Celebrate with
Tiana and Jasmine

Let's discover more about princess celebrations in Agrabah and New Orleans ...

New Friends

When Jasmine's father holds royal events, Jasmine enjoys meeting guests from faraway lands.

Magical Music

Tiana loves music. Her friend Louis is always happy to play the trumpet at her princess parties.

Celebration Food

Tiana is a brilliant cook. She held a big celebration when she opened her restaurant, Tiana's Palace.

Add some pretty colours to this picture.

Enchanting Puzzles

Join Jasmine and Tiana in their magical worlds to complete these princess puzzles.

Odd One Out

Look closely at the pictures below. Can you circle the odd one out in each row?

1

a   b   c

2

a   b   c

3

a   b   c

Special Delivery

Tiana has received an invitation to a ball.
Use the key to work out who it's from.

Dear Tiana,

I would like to invite you
to join me at the palace ball.

Love from

Key

e   v   a   o   n

Which letter from the key doesn't appear in the name?

Pretty Scarves

Jasmine loves wearing colourful scarves. Which two scarves match exactly?

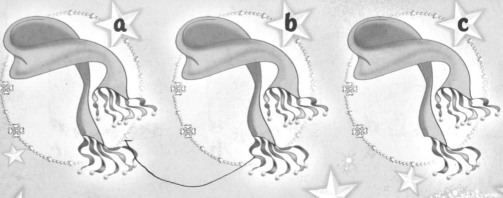

a   b   c

Answers on page 67.

Celebrate with
Ariel

40

Ariel loves music and singing. Her underwater celebrations are filled with laughter and fun ...

Family Fun

Ariel enjoys planning parties for King Triton and her six sisters. They always have lots of fun together.

Musical Friend

Ariel loves music. Her friend Sebastian conducts the orchestra at Ariel's underwater parties.

Colour Ariel and Prince Eric as they dance.

Party Time

Ariel uses things she finds in the sea to make party decorations.

The Lost Voices

Read this exciting Ariel story. When you see a picture, say the right word.

King Triton

Ursula

shell necklace

Sebastian

One day, Ariel's sisters were rehearsing for 's birthday concert.

Little did they know that, as they sang,  was secretly sucking their beautiful voices into her enchanted .

When Ariel arrived later, she found that her sisters had lost their voices.

"There's only one person responsible for this," said Ariel. "!"

Ariel led her sisters to 's lair, where the sea witch was boasting:

"With their voices trapped in this shell, 's concert will be ruined!"

"I think  needs a taste of her own medicine," Ariel whispered.

When  wasn't looking, Ariel poured sleeping potion into the sea witch's goblet. It wasn't long before  drank the potion and fell into a deep sleep.

42

Ariel quickly took the  and swam back to the palace. But when she got there, the shell wouldn't open!

"We need something special to break the spell," she said.

Just then, Ariel heard   's band practising. "That's it!" she cried.

Ariel gathered all the musicians in the kingdom and asked them to play together. The magic of the music broke the spell! The shell opened and the mermaids' voices returned, just in time.

"When you work together, magic happens!" said Ariel, happily.

The End

43

Ocean Gifts

Some gifts have been delivered! Follow the trails to find out which present is for which friend.

a  **b** **c**

Can you spot the starfish hidden on the page.

Ariel

Flounder

Sebastian

Answers on page 68.

Underwater Fun

Join the dots to finish drawing the seahorse, then colour this happy scene.

• 1

• 2

• 3

• 20

• 11

10 • • 12

19 • • 4

9 • • 8 • 13

• 5 7 •

• 6 • 14

• 18

15 •

17 • 16 •

How many fish can you spot on this page?

Royal Concert

Ariel is the star attraction of this underwater concert.

1 How many Mer people is Ariel singing for? Trace the right answer.

6 or 7

2 Point to the sister who is clapping.

s o n g

3 What's the word in the bubbles?

S o n g

4 What instrument is the octopus playing?

A piano ✓

A trumpet

5 Tick the shell when you spot this singing fish.

Celebrate with
Aurora

The fairies help make Aurora's celebrations truly magical. Let's find out how ...

Pretty in Pink

Aurora likes dressing-up for royal events. Her favourite outfit is her pink ball gown with a gold tiara.

Add some pretty colours to this picture.

Woodland Friends

Aurora loves to dance. She enjoys ballroom dancing, ballet and dancing with her animal friends in the forest.

Perfect Prince

Royal balls wouldn't be the same for Aurora without Prince Phillip. He always makes her feel special.

A Starry Night

1 Aurora was getting ready for a romantic evening with Prince Phillip, but she couldn't decide what to wear.

2 Just then, her fairy friends appeared. "We have a present for you," they said, waving their wands to make a spinning wheel appear.

3 Aurora used the spinning wheel to weave some pretty cloth. Then her animal friends helped her make it into a beautiful dress.

4 Later, that evening, Aurora and Prince Phillip enjoyed a delicious meal under the stars. "This is lovely," Aurora said.

5 Then, Aurora and Prince Phillip went for a moonlit walk. As they danced together, sparks of light flew from Aurora's dress. "It's magical!" she gasped.

6 They watched in amazement as the sparks from the dress became stars and formed a picture in the sky. "Now this night will last forever!" sighed Aurora.

The End

Love Song

Prince Phillip and Aurora are singing a love song. Add some pretty colours to this picture.

How many musical notes can you count?

5

Answer on page 68.

Party Hat

Make and wear this princess hat to look like a true fairy tale princess.

1 Take a piece of white card and bend it into a cone shape to fit your head. Secure in place with sticky tape.

2 Decorate by covering the cone in gold shiny paper.

Match the colour of your hat to your outfit.

3 Curl pieces of gold ribbon and attach them to the top of the cone. Glue sequins on in a pretty pattern.

4 Cut a piece of netting, no longer than the height of the hat. Thread one end into the top of the hat and glue in place. Use hair grips to secure your hat on your head.

You will need:

gold paper and white card

sequins

scissors

glue

sticky tape

gold ribbon

netting

Ask an adult to help.

53

Princess Puzzles

Join in the fun with Aurora by completing these exciting princess activities.

Mirror Message

Aurora has written a secret message for you.

ƨǝiɈɿɒq ƨƨǝɔniɿᑫ
.lɒɔipɒm ǝɿɒ

Hold this page up to a mirror to reveal what it says.

Perfect Pairs

a

b

c

Can you help Aurora match these party shoes into pairs?

f

e

d

Flower Maze

Help to guide Prince Phillip
through the maze to Aurora.

Start

Finish

How many flowers
will he pick for
his princess along
the way?

Answers on page 68.

55

Celebrate with
Snow White

Like all princesses, Snow White loves having parties with all of her friends. Sounds like fun!

Time for Tea

Snow White likes baking cakes and biscuits ... and the dwarfs like eating them at Snow White's tea parties!

Picnic Parties

Snow White and the dwarfs often have picnics in the forest. The woodland creatures join them too.

Starlit Dance

The Prince and Snow White enjoy a dance whenever they can. Snow White loves dancing under the stars.

Colour Snow White and her prince.

The Forest Princess

Read this lovely tale about Snow White and her forest friends.

One sunny day, Snow White decided to go for a walk in the forest. As she skipped along merrily, she suddenly noticed a beautiful tiara hanging from a tree.

The tiara was made from twigs and flowers. As Snow White took it from the tree, she noticed it had something written on it. "Property of the Forest Princess," Snow White read.

"Oh dear," thought Snow White. "This Forest Princess must have lost her tiara. I need to find her and return it."

So, Snow White headed to the dwarfs' cottage to ask them if they knew where the forest princess lived. But the dwarfs had never heard of her.

Next, Snow White went to the palace to ask the Prince about the Forest Princess. But the Prince didn't know who she was either.

Snow White decided to make a poster to hang in the forest with a drawing of the tiara on it. "Hopefully the Forest Princess will see it," she said.

All of a sudden, a naughty squirrel grabbed the tiara out of Snow White's

hand and scampered off. "Oh, no!" cried Snow White. "How will the Forest Princess get her tiara back now?"

As Snow White said these words, some birds flew down and gently placed the tiara on her head.

Suddenly, all of the forest creatures appeared and Snow White realised that she was the Forest Princess! The tiara was the forest's thank you gift to her for taking care of it so well.

Snow White was very touched by the gesture. "Seeing as everyone is here and I have a new tiara to wear, we should have a celebration," she told her friends.

So Snow White and the forest creatures danced and sang. Everyone had a wonderful time, especially the new Forest Princess!

The End

59

Princess Teasers

Use a little bit of princess magic to help you solve these fun puzzles.

Let's Celebrate!

Can you find the party words below in this wordsearch? Words go down and across.

P	R	E	S	E	N	T	R	W	N
E	T	F	S	T	Y	U	B	I	R
B	U	E	T	E	R	C	A	K	E
E	I	O	V	F	I	B	L	H	N
R	E	G	A	B	Y	O	L	I	C
M	U	S	I	C	I	J	O	L	E
D	F	A	K	Y	N	W	O	Y	S
N	E	D	A	N	C	I	N	G	S
C	Q	A	R	U	O	T	V	E	A
Z	S	M	A	G	I	C	O	L	B

DANCING ♡ MUSIC ♡

BALLOON ♡ PRESENT ♡

CAKE ♡

Tick a heart as you find each word.

60

Which one of these shadows matches this picture of Snow White perfectly?

a

b

c

d

Ring Jumble

Snow White is sorting out her jewellery. How many rings can you count?

Write your answer here.

Tea Party Puzzle

The friends are enjoying a tea party.
Which jigsaw piece completes the scene?

a

b

c

d

e

Write your
answer here.

62

Answer on page 68.

Royal Dance

Snow White and the prince are dancing at a party.
Add some pretty colours to the picture.

Can you spot this cake?

Party Time

The princesses are having a party!
Join in the fun with these activities.

Royal Invitation

Which of these party
invitations is the biggest?

a

b

c

d

Princess Accessory

What is Tiana taking to the
party? Join the dots to find out.

Add some pretty
colours to finish
Tiana's accessory.

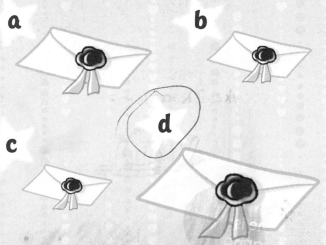

Party Present

a

Cinderella's bird friends are bringing her a present. Can you spot three differences in picture b?

b

Pretty Cakes

Which princess has baked these cupcakes? Read the clues to find out.

She is wearing a tiara.

She doesn't have black hair.

She is holding a rose.

Tick the heart next to the correct princess.

Make sure you complete these puzzles before cutting out the poster on the next page!

Answers on page 68.

Answers

Page 16

Princess Present
Gift c.

Pages 18-19

Royal Celebration
Colourful Gown: pink.
Jewel Maze:

Two yellow jewels.
Odd One Out: c.

Page 24

Magical Message
I love surprises.
The dress is purple and pink.

Page 25

Pretty Rapunzel
Flowers b and d.

Page 27

Lovely Lights

Page 32

Magical Match
d doesn't appear in the picture.

Page 33

Belle's Ball Gown
Mrs Potts and Chip are hiding
behind the Wardobe.

Pages 34-35

Enchanted Ballroom
1. 8.
2. Dancing.
3. a and b.
4. The book is on the footstool.
5. 5 red petals.

Pages 38-39

Enchanting Puzzles
Odd One Out:
1 – a, 2 – c, 3 – b.
Special Delivery:
The invitation is
from Naveen.
o doesn't appear
in the name.
Pretty Scarves:
Scarves a and b
match exactly.

Page 44

Ocean Gifts

a - Ariel, b - Sebastian, c - Flounder.

Page 45

Underwater Fun

There are 4 fish
(don't forget Flounder!)

Pages 46-47

Royal Concert

1. Ariel is singing for 7 Mer people.
3. song.
4. A piano.

Page 52

Love Song

There are 5 muscial notes.

Pages 54-55

Princess Puzzles

Mirror Message: Princess parties are magical.
Perfect Pairs: a and d, b and f, c and e.

Flower Maze: Prince Phillip will pick 6 flowers along the way.

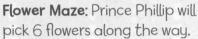

Pages 60-61

Princess Teasers

Let's Celebrate!:

Shadow Match: c.
Ring Jumble: There are 9 rings.

Page 62

Tea Party Puzzle

Jigsaw piece b.

Pages 64-65

Party Time

Royal Invitation: d.
Princess Accessory: A handbag.
Party Present:

Pretty Cakes: Belle.